P9-ELW-702

Financial Insanity[SM]

How to Keep Wall Street's Cancer From Spreading To Your Portfolio

by DAVID J. SCRANTON

CLU, ChFC, CFP®, CFA, MSFS

(in collaboration with M.G. Crisci)

Orca Publishing Company
Carlsbad, CA 92011

Designed by Good World Media
Edited by Raymond and Lucille Mancini
Illustrations by Erin Kelly

Manufactured in the United States of America

Library of Congress Control No.
2011927334

ISBN 978-0-9834478-0-1

This book is dedicated to Albert Einstein.

**"Insanity is doing the same thing,
over and over again, but
expecting different results."**

Preface

My name is David Scranton.

For the past 24 years, I have been helping investors of all ages plan for retirement. For the first half of my career, like most financial advisors, I leaned on the stock market as a primary tool to help clients grow their money. For the second half of my career, I learned how to protect and grow their retirement wealth the old-fashioned way: by focusing on financial tools that generate the income they need to live a pleasant, stress-free retirement.

So, what happened at the mid-way point in my career that caused me to change? One event: The tech stock boom. During the late 1990's, I grew more and more concerned that the stock market bubble was going to burst. I didn't have a crystal ball, so I didn't know when it would happen but common sense told me that it would happen. I began to lose sleep at night, concerned about my clients' retirement money, so I knew I had to make a change.

Recently, I was being interviewed and was asked, "What is the one thing in your career that you are most proud of?" I paused and pondered and responded, "Unlike many advisors, I had the courage to change my business model when I knew that the old stock market based model was no longer in the best interest of my clients."

As you can see from the title page, I have spent a lifetime educating myself, so I can better educate my clients. I hold a Master's Degree in Financial Planning; I am a Chartered Financial Consultant, a

Chartered Life Underwriter, a Chartered Financial Analyst, and a Certified Financial Planner®.

I've spoken to tens of thousands of people over the years about my philosophies and processes and built a thriving financial practice in New England with hundreds of satisfied clients. During that period, people have told me some of the most incredible stories about what they have been advised to do with their retirement money. I call these recommendations *Financial Insanity* because they have little or no basis in how the financial markets work—past, present, or future.

Hence, the goal of this book is to explain and educate you—in simple, plain English–how the stock market really works, and will continue to work, in the hopes that you'll make better, more informed decisions when it comes to investing your hard-earned assets.

I will also share with you an investment strategy that delivers peace of mind and works, regardless of market conditions. Your retirement assets will generate predictable income year after year without the risks of the stock market. This income can be reinvested if retirement is still a few years down the road.

For your reading convenience, I've also tried to make each chapter succinct and entertaining. The book also breaks into three distinct parts: The Facts, The Bull, and The Reality. Enjoy.

Table of Contents

\

Part 2 – Cont'd

Part 3 – The Reality

Part One

The Facts

Looking at historical stock market trends.

Chapter 1

Ignoring Defense

"Offense sells tickets; Defense wins championships"
~Paul "Bear" Bryant

Think about some of the great sports dynasties of all times: The Green Bay Packers under Vince Lombardi, the Boston Celtics under Red Auerbach, and the New York Yankees under Joe Torre. They all knew how to score runs or points, but they all started with the premise that a strong defense made their offense better. In other words, they protected their downside, year after year. The players understood the objective was to increase their odds of winning game after game, and so did the coaches who advised, prodded, and cajoled the players to excellence. Building a smart financial plan that works year after year is a lot like building that championship sports franchise. Know when to reach for the stars, but make sure you always, and I mean always, protect your downside, because if the base erodes, it takes a long time to rebuild.

So, let's begin our journey to financial sanity by talking about the stock market. Suppose you were invested in the market during a down cycle and happen to lose 50 percent of your portfolio value. Do you have any idea how much your portfolio has to bounce back just to break even? Do you know how many years that could take? Has your investment advisor ever discussed that possibility with you?

Rebuilding to Zero

As you can see from the following chart, if your portfolio loses 50 percent of its value, you need to earn a whopping 100 percent merely to break-even! People just seem to forget if they start with $100 and lose $50, they have to double the remaining $50 just to get back to $100. Earning 50 percent only gets you to $75, so you're still shy $25.

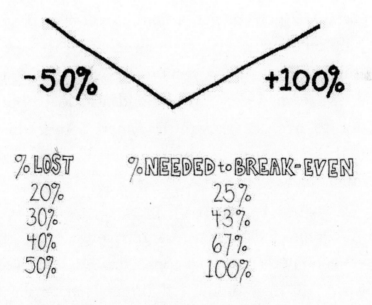

% LOST   % NEEDED to BREAK-EVEN
20%   25%
30%   43%
40%   67%
50%   100%

During the 1990s, most financial advisors and market "experts" implied that some of the bigger losses this chart paints are unrealistic and bleak, with low odds of actually ever happening. My response ...that is patently untrue! Since the year 2000, the market has experienced two drops of 50 percent from prior highs, in the periods of 2000-2003 and 2007-2009.

Time to Recover

Losing 50 percent of your portfolio is only half the story. You also need to consider the time it takes to recover that wealth. For example, if you earn a respectable 7 percent per annum, it will take 10 years to fully recover. If you assume a heady 10 percent return, it will still take 7 years to recover. During that time, you earned zero growth and also lost opportunities to achieve growth elsewhere. And, there's more bad news: when considering inflation, your total wealth actually regressed.

As seen in the chart on page 13, from 2003 to 2007, certain lucky investors recovered from their previous 50 percent loss in approximately 4 1/2 years. However, if they didn't sell immediately after the recovery, then they were not so lucky! Stocks began another down cycle, and prior gains were again diminished.

The Misguided Cheerleader

So, how is it that many intelligent investors failed to liquidate in 2007 after recovering their losses? For some, perhaps it was a misguided sense of optimism. In other cases, perhaps their investment advisor was filling the role of a misguided cheerleader.

Think about it...As you recovered your losses, did your investment broker call to tell you to take your gains and go, or did he imply the market should go even higher?

Then, as the market began to drop again in 2008, did you call your advisor to share your concerns? Did he again suggest you "hang in there" because things were at or near the bottom?

As the market dropped even further, were you wishing you had followed your instincts and cut your losses?

As you will see in the following chapters, history repeats itself again, again, and again. And, investment brokers appear either unable or unwilling to accept the lessons of history.

The Personal Effect

"The first rule is not to lose. The second rule is not to forget the first rule"

~Warren Buffet

If you were unfortunate enough not to take the sage advice of the world's most successful investor,

Warren Buffet, you probably had to do some belt tightening during the past decade.

Did you postpone retirement and maybe push back Social Security till 65 or 67 to get higher pay-outs?

Did you have to get a part-time job to generate additional income to offset lost interest on your investments?

Did you have to postpone any decisions on major purchases? Perhaps you kept that car a little longer than you planned.

Did you delay/modify a planned vacation?

Did you think twice before spending on those little extras?

In retrospect, planning defensively doesn't sound so bad. Does it?

Chapter 2

Stock Market Biorhythms

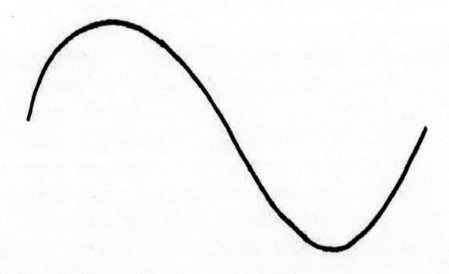

"Over the long run, the stock market outperforms other asset classes."

~Mr. Average Advisor

Have you ever asked your broker how long is "the long run?" If you haven't, then allow me to answer that question for you. But first, I need to ask you a question:

Do you believe generally speaking that history repeats itself more often than not?

Personally, I do believe that history repeats itself, especially when it comes to the stock market. Let me explain.

You've probably heard, read or been told that the stock market traditionally delivers about a 10 percent average return over the long, long term. But, that "average" is actually the sum of two "averages." Over time, 7 to 8 percent of that long term return comes from price appreciation; the remainder, 2 to 3 percent, comes from dividends.

$$10\% = (7\text{-}8\%) + (2\text{-}3\%)$$
TOTAL RETURN   GROWTH   DIVIDENDS

The Real Story

However, as you are about to learn, those averages can be misleading. Let me explain. Imagine two friends are jogging buddies. They tell you that they average 15 miles a week. But, upon examining their exercise routine further you discover the real story: one gentleman is an exercise nut who runs 30 miles a week, and the other is a couch potato who prefers watching professional football. Technically, they still average 15 miles a week, but the details paint a very different picture of real performance.

The "real story" of the stock market is much the same. History tells us that the 7 to 8 percent long term average growth rate actually comes in clumps. There are long periods of time where the market experiences zero growth—absolutely nothing, zilch, nada—and long periods where the market averages 12 to 15 percent growth. To use Wall Street lingo, there were times when the stock market slept like a bear and then ran like a bull. Let me demonstrate by showing you the last 100 years.

0% GROWTH	12-15% GROWTH
1899-1921	1921-1929
1929-1954	1954-1966
1966-1982	1982-2000
2000-???	TBD

As you can see, the actual periods on the left were periods of flat performance. That doesn't mean, for example, that during the 1899 to 1921 period the stock market declined for 22 straight years. There were good and bad years, but history is very clear here. The good years and bad years washed each other out, resulting in zero net growth for 22 years.

In fact, during the last century, the stock market had flat performance accompanied by extreme market volatility over 50 percent of the time. It's also worth noting that the second greatest bull market of the last century occurred just before the Great Depression.

The Longer View

Now, if by some chance, you're a statistical nut like me, you may wonder what stock market cycles looked like before 1900. The answer is that they were about the same: We consistently had 15-20 year bull markets, followed by 15-20 year bear markets. Some of the bull markets were a bit shorter, but virtually all of the bear markets lasted 15-20 years.

As you can imagine, getting information about the markets during the nineteenth century was not easy. The only information that was readily available to me and most other investment brokers during the 1990's was from 1926 to the present.

In fact, in the late 1990s, it was fashionable for most brokers to show their clients what I affectionately refer to as the "mountain chart." It's that chart which shows how the stock market has grown from 1926 to the present. When stepping back and observing from afar, it was quite impressive that so many brokers learned to use this as a sales tool.

Historical stock market facts that predate 1926 are much harder to locate. I know because when I started doing my research in the 1990's, I had to uncover and interpret raw data.

How Long is Long-Term?

History suggests a full bull-bear market cycle is 35 years. Statistically, that means that over a 35-year period, the stock market should outperform all other asset classes. What does that mean for investors?

Any money you know you will not need for the next 35 years could be invested in the stock market.

How old will you be 35 years from now?

What's Next?

It's now 2011, and I have two questions for you: Do you think that today's bear market will reverse nearly 200 years of stock market history? Do you think today's bear market will end after only 11 years? Anything's possible; after all the Boston Red Sox won the World Series, not once, but twice! But, history is clearly trying to tell us that the market could be "stuck in the muck" for another 10 years or so.

"Those who don't know history
are destined to repeat it."
~Edmund Burke

Chapter 3

Demystifying Double-Talk

"I have never lied to you.
I have always told you some version of the truth."
~Jack Nicholson as
"Harry" in the movie
"Something's Gotta Give"

Wall Street loves to use complicated lingo that can overwhelm the average investor. Consequently, I need to explain, clarify, and turn into simple, plain English, the concept of Secular versus Cyclical Market Cycles.

When you watch a market analyst on TV, how long does he generally imply a bear market lasts: two–three years? It is sometimes less but rarely more.

As you can see from the preceding chapters, history indicates that a bear market typically runs 15 – 20 years or longer. The question becomes, who is right and who is wrong? Can both of us be right? Do you think that there can be different interpretations of the same history?

The answer lies in how you define a bear market. So, let's take a look at the "facts" of the last long-term bear market, 1966 to 1982.

Versions of the Truth

Again, I do believe that history does repeat itself, although, when it comes to the stock market, there are too many "versions of the truth." Let me explain.

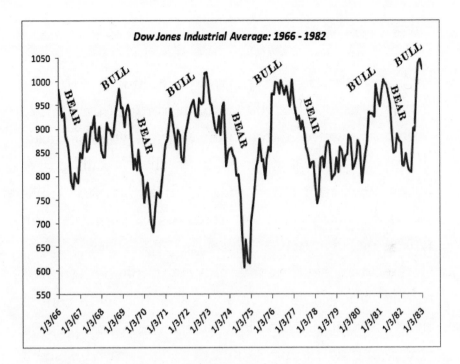

Dow Jones Industrial Average: 1966 - 1982

The cycles I labeled on this graph are what your typical analyst would call textbook bear and bull markets. They are often referred to by the industry as "cyclical" or short-term trends. But my clients tell me almost daily that in the real world, when their hard-earned dollars experience zero growth for 16 years, it's really one big bear market cycle. So based upon my real world definition, a "secular" or long term bear market cycle averages 15-20 years or longer.

Bear Market Rallies?

Within every secular bull or bear market, there are cyclical cycles. For example, at the end of 2010, the market was up over 80 percent from its bottom 21 months earlier in March 2009. History would indicate that we were experiencing a "cyclical" bull market inside of a long-term "secular" bear market. Times like these are often referred to as "compression rallies" or "bear market rallies."

Another way to think about this phenomenon is to think about a home in a warm climate with central air conditioning. Now, imagine you've placed a space heater in one of the rooms. You've created a small pocket of warmth in the area immediately sur-rounding the space heater. But once you leave that small area, the air conditioning will *dominate* the overall space.

Selling Optimism

Given the above, why is it that Wall Street prefers to speak in terms of textbook cyclical instead of real world secular cycles? As we will discuss in later chap-ters, how likely would you be to invest in the stock market if Wall Street told you a bear market was upon us and would persist for years?

Simply put, focusing on shorter-term cyclical cycles allows Wall Street to speak optimistically more often. It knows that people are simply more likely to invest when they are optimistic and think the markets are going up.

Chapter 4

Understanding Basics

"Price is what you pay.
Value is what you get."

~Warren Buffet

Why the illustration? What's a kid in baggy pants got to do with the stock market?

Suppose you buy a pair of pants that is a little too big for your child or grandchild. You've got two choices: shrink the pants down to size or hold them until the child grows into them.

The same options apply when the price of stocks gets overinflated in relation to annual corporate profits. The stocks get baggy. That brings me to my observations in 1998. As a practicing financial advisor, I was starting to get concerned about the fact that the average price of stocks in the market was overinflated relative to actual corporate profits. I knew from my studies of market history and understanding of basic financial ratios that one of two things had to happen. Overall stock prices could shrink by 75 percent, resulting in a Dow Jones Industrial Average below 3,000. Or, we could slip into a period of significant and prolonged volatility while we waited for corporate profits to grow into the new overinflated price levels. I just wasn't sure when the party would be over.

The Basic Ratios

Why was I so confident about my predictions in the late 90's? I had an understanding of a stock market staple: price to earnings ratio. Every stock has a price to earnings ratio, as does the entire stock market. The formula is relatively simple:

P/E = Price per Share/Earnings per Share

As a very general rule if you are comparing two stocks in the same industry, the one with the lower ratio is probably the better "buy" because it is considered to be "undervalued." For example:

COMPANY A: THE STOCK PRICE IS $30 A SHARE
CORPORATE EARNINGS ARE $1/SHARE

COMPANY B: THE STOCK PRICE IS $50 A SHARE
CORPORATE EARNINGS ARE $5/SHARE

Which one is the better value? Company B, because it has a P/E of 10 compared to Company A's P/E of 30.

COMPANY A: P/E=$30/$1=30
COMPANY B: P/E=$50/$5=10

Note: This illustration is merely a conceptual example. In the real world, the question of which stock is a better investment is more complex because of a number of other factors.

Average P/E ratios of stocks in the overall stock market can also be a good indicator of when stock market levels are generally too high and ready for a drop. This was the case in the late 1990's when average P/E ratios had exceeded 30. In other words, each dollar invested was buying 3 cents of earnings or annual profits (1/30 = 3.3). Put another way, you were earning about 3 percent when you could have taken the same money and bought an FDIC insured CD back then with no risk that was paying 5 percent.

To illustrate how ridiculous buying behavior was during the late 90's, I'd like you to consider the following. You have decided to purchase an ice cream parlor business. The owner wants $3 million. When you check the books and records, you discover the business makes $100,000 annually. In other words, the business's P/E ratio is 30; it will take you 30 years to recoup your cost. Keep in mind, at the same time you could have bought government bonds that would have returned more without scooping a single scoop of ice cream. Would you have bought the business?

P/E Ratios and Market History

What does history tell us about P/E ratios? When we've come to the end of a secular bull market like the late 1990's, P/E ratios are typically near or above 30. Historically, this is a signal that we are about to slide into a secular bear market that could last 15-20 years or longer.

The good news is that at the end of a secular bear market, P/E ratios typically slip below 10, often into the 6-8 range. Historically, this signals the beginning of the next secular bull market cycle.

Why do secular bear markets last 15 to 20 years or longer? That's how long it takes P/E ratios to drop from over 30 into the 6–8 range. Again, this can happen in one of two ways: Stock market levels can drop by 75 percent—this seldom happens. Or, corporate earnings can quadruple so that they grow into the inflated prices, much like the child needs to grow into his baggy pants. How long does it take for corporate earnings to quadruple? You guessed it, 15 – 20 years or longer.

Chapter 5

The Human Factor

*"Each generation imagines itself to be more intelligent
than the one that went before it,
and wiser than the one that comes after it."*

~George Orwell

Remember when you were a kid, life was simple? You wanted to learn how to ride a bike and your parents helped you.

Then you got older and wiser. You were earning money. Again, I bet they tried to give you advice because they wanted you to avoid some of the mistakes they made. Did they waste their breath?

One day, you were a parent, and you tried to pass on some financially sound advice to your children. What happened then? Did you waste your breath?

For better or worse, *The Human Factor* seems to cause each generation to learn only from its own mistakes. Unfortunately, this almost universal axiom really seems to apply to investment mistakes. The primary mistake we are most concerned about in this book is every generation's tendency to create its own speculative stock market bubble. In fact, this tendency is one of the primary reasons why secular bull and bear markets last so long.

Let's face it. There are two basic emotions that control people's investment decisions: fear and greed. When times appear good, optimism abounds, and our greed kicks in. We want to make more and more, so we invest longer than common sense suggests. As

P/E ratios climb higher and higher, the press and your investment broker spin the never-ending merry-go-round of optimism ever faster. Human nature drives us to make irrational market decisions. Then, suddenly, one day the merry-go-round comes to a sudden stop. The market starts to drop, and doom and gloom set in. As the market continues to drop, our fears kick in and we become paralyzed. Our investments slide. We lose some or much of what we made.

The longer the good times roll, the more over-valued the stock market becomes, the larger the investment bubble becomes, and the greater the length and depth of the inevitable market contraction.

The 35 Years

At what age did you start getting serious about paying attention to the markets and your retirement investments? If you're like most people who respond to this question, the answer is somewhere in the mid-forties or even later. There are lots of reasons: mortgage payments, college costs for the kids, family vacations, etc.

Since the average life expectancy these days is around 80, that means the average investor will be paying attention to the financial markets for the last 35 years of his or her life. By any chance, do you remember how long history suggests most secular bull-bear market cycles last? That's right, 35 years.

So, just when you lived through an entire 35-year cycle as an active investor, you're at your life expectancy. You're just starting to understand it is part of a natural bio-rhythm or market cycle, but, in some ways, it's too late to do much about it.

Interestingly, the market is not the only thing that experiences generational cycles. Think about the history of war during the last century: World War I, World War II, Vietnam, and now Iraq. Why did history repeat itself every 30-35 years? I believe that it is because each generation had to learn its own lessons in its own way. Do you remember when we left Vietnam we vowed to never get into another war without an exit strategy? Then along came Iraq.

My purpose in writing this book is simple: I want to help you understand the natural order of market biorhythms without your having to live through the entire market cycle. I want you to stop the *Financial*

Insanity: i.e., periods of zero growth accompanied by significant portfolio volatility.

Chapter 6

The Fallacy of Buy & Hold

*...buy and hold doesn't work
in a market like this.*

~Warren Buffet

During the 1980's and 1990's, Wall Street told you the best investment strategy was to "buy and hold." We were taught that trying to time the market would lead to underperformance. It proved to be good advice because, in retrospect, we were in the midst of the best secular bull market our country has ever known. In general, "buy and hold" works well in an upward trending market.

Let's fast forward to the 21st Century. The account of the average "buy and hold" investor between December 31, 1999 and December 31, 2010 is down in value or, at best, break even. Over that period, the Standard & Poor's 500 Index (a compendium of 500 of America's most stable companies) dropped approximately 20 percent in value. Why? Because this period represented the beginning of a secular bear market, which by definition means a no growth period over a long, long time. So, by utilizing a "buy and hold" strategy over this period, you were participating in this part of the cycle's natural movement (biorhythm), resulting in a negative rate of return.

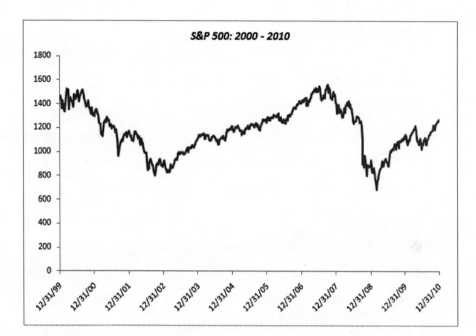

S&P 500: 2000 - 2010

Despite the above chart, do you know why Wall Street still recommends a "buy and hold" strategy for most investors? The bottom line is self-interest. If you take money out of the market for a year or two, it cannot generate fees on your account. During that time, Wall Street's profits will drop and so will the investment broker's income.

The story is much the same for mutual fund managers. If large sums of money exit the fund, their fees will also plummet. Additionally, for reasons beyond the scope of this book, the performance of investments under their control will suffer.

Real Options

There are only two potential strategies to make money in a long-term, secular bear market:

The first is "Sector Selection." Even during the most severe general market declines, there are certain business sectors that will outperform the pack. If you are able to pick those sectors, you will at least have a chance of making a return on your money. Although this strategy sounds good in theory, it is extremely difficult to implement, even for market professionals. After all, when the tide goes out, all the boats drop.

The second strategy that can work in a secular bear market is "Timing the Market." Even in this part of the market cycle, there are periodic, short-term cyclical bull markets. By making wholesale moves into and out of the market, you have potential opportunities to buy low and sell high.

However, timing the market does involve a significant degree of risk...even for investment professionals. For those of you approaching or in retirement, you need to ask yourself, "At this stage of my life, how much of my money do I want to expose to a risky strategy like timing the market?"

If you're like most people seeking an enjoyable, worry free retirement, your response would typically be "not much."

There is a third option that we'll touch on later in this book, but it runs counter to what Wall Street says: "Always have at least a portion of your assets in the market, regardless of cycles." Its rationale is that people are living longer these days, so they need a hedge against inflation over the long term.

However, I dare you to find an investment textbook which says that the stock market represents a good inflation hedge. It's a fallacy created by Wall Street during the go-go 80's and 90's. Traditionally, only commodities and tangible assets, such as real estate and gold, were considered an adequate hedge against inflation.

Besides, I'd like to ask you....does getting zero growth on your money for 15 or 20 years in a secular bear market sound like a good inflation hedge?

I would suggest there may be another philosophy. It would actually be better to place your money in a mattress than lose money in a secular bear market. Now don't get me wrong, I'm not recommending the mattress approach, but there is no law that says you must have any money in the stock market. You can make money without investing in the stock market.

Chapter 7

Biorhythms
vs. Business Cycles

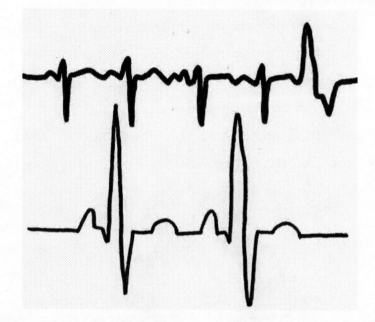

"Get the facts, or the facts will get you. And when you get 'em, get 'em right, or they will get you wrong."

~Thomas Fuller

Although dramatically different, investors and their advisors frequently confuse business or economic cycles with stock market BioRhythms. This mistake can be extremely detrimental to your financial health. Why? You can make the wrong investment decisions based on an analysis of the wrong set of real facts.

Business Cycles

Most people are confident that they understand the concept of business cycles. Are you aware that these typically last only seven to eight years? These cycles also tend to have their own pattern: typically they go from recession to recovery and back to recession, as highlighted below:

Stock Market Biorhythms

On the other hand, stock market cycles usually take 35 years to complete a full circle or one full Biorhythm. Simply put, there are usually four or five complete business cycles in one complete stock market Biorhythm. That's why during a 15 or 20 year secular *bull* market, the economy will inevitably have *bad* business cycles. Ironically, due to a variety of factors that I'll discuss, the optimism inherent in bull market biorhythms always seems to overpower the reality of the bad times.

Similarly, during a 15-20 secular *bear* market cycle, there will inevitably be some *good* economic times. Ironically, the pessimism inherent in a bear market biorhythm seems to generally overpower the reality of the good times.

The Role of Government

As most people know, the role of the Federal Reserve is to maintain a vital American economy. At the beginning of a recession, it lowers interest rates to stimulate economic growth. Conversely, during periods of economic recovery, the Fed typically raises interest rates to avoid economic overstimulation and inflationary spikes.

Unknowingly, the Federal government also plays a part in creating undue or unwarranted optimism. During secular bear market cycles–like the present– we often hear the government saying that we are emerging from a recession and heading into a period of recovery. Predictably, such pronouncements make investors optimistic. They begin investing more, and the stock market rises. It might go up for a while, but if we're still in a secular bear market, it is likely to take another plunge, causing some of your prized investments to shrink.

Obviously the Fed is not intentionally trying to have its citizens lose their hard-earned assets. So why does this happen again and again? Unfortunately, investors often interpret the Fed's pronouncements as leading to a *stock market recovery*. They confuse short-term business cycles with long term stock market biorhythms.

To make matters worse, Wall Street and its investment brokers typically jump on the "recovery" bandwagon, also. Why? As discussed earlier, The Street prefers to talk about cyclical stock market cycles instead of secular stock market cycles because it gets to speak optimistically more often. It's only logical then that Wall Street prefers to reinforce Fed economic recovery pronouncements because, again it can speak optimistically more often.

The Biggest Losers

Who is the ultimate victim of all this optimism? You, the average investor! You've been duped into believing that all is well again, just before the next shoe is about to drop.

To some extent, human error is a non-controllable market force that extends way beyond the financial battlefield. One only needs to look at the tragic lessons of Vietnam.

We had better armed and trained soldiers and more of them. We didn't understand, though, that the Viet Cong had changed the rules. Legions of brave, young men went into the jungles to seek and destroy the Cong who were hidden in underground passages. Unfortunately, there were always more passages where they could hide and regroup, where sheer force and conventional weaponry were ineffective. We made terrible human investments by analyzing the wrong set of facts.

Chapter 8

Waves of Capitulation

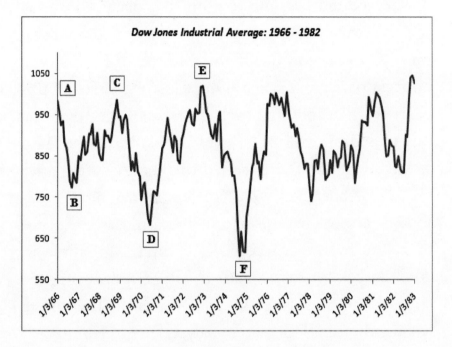

Dow Jones Industrial Average: 1966 - 1982

"All truth passes through three stages. First, it is ridiculed. Second, it is violently opposed. Third, it is accepted as being self-evident."

~Arthur Schopenhauer

Remember the secular bear market of 1966 to 1982 that we examined back in Chapter 3? I'd like to spend a few minutes discussing the periodic drops that occurred within that cycle, the "waves", so to speak. Please refer to the graph on page 53.

Notice the first major drop that occurred during this 16 year cycle (A to B). Now look at the second drop (C to D) and finally the third (E to F). Did you notice a pattern? What you have just witnessed in this chart is the reality that each drop was larger than the previous drop causing "waves" of anxiety. The third was the biggest. There were drops that occurred after the third, but they were smaller in magnitude. Although a wave pattern like this doesn't always occur in a secular bear market, it is common for these to come in sets of threes with the third drop being the largest. This phenomenon tends to rear its head more frequently than Wall Street analysts care to admit.

As you can tell from my tone, waves may make pretty charts, but they are not positive phenomena when it comes to either your money or your psyche as an investor.

There are lots of so-called "wave theories" that attempt to explain this phenomenon, most of which are extremely complicated. I'd like to give you what I believe is the simplest explanation that you'll ever hear. You might be wondering, "Why bother?" Understanding what causes these waves is central to my philosophy that there is a smarter investment strategy that can earn predictable income without requiring you to ride these waves.

The First Wave

Look to the left of the graph when the first drop occurred. That was generally considered the end of the good times. It's at the end of a secular bull market cycle. During that previous bull market cycle, market dips were short and not terribly severe.

Wall Street advised you to "hang in there and don't sell." Conventional wisdom explained, "You can't time the market." As a result, when the first market drop occurred, many investors acted like wooden soldiers. They dutifully sat on the sidelines and held. The market recovered and the mini-crisis was averted. Investors then experienced a period of market calm. The pro-market prognosticators smiled.

The Second Wave

Several years passed. Some bad news arrived which caused the beginning of another drop. During good times, this bad news would have manifested itself as merely a blip in the stock market. This time, though, several years had passed during which investors became frustrated with market losses and/or lack of expected gains. Many became impatient. The average investor started to sell, which caused the market to slide into a second period of decline during the *same* secular bear market cycle. Because there were more people selling into this second drop, the second drop was, as is often the case, bigger than the first.

The Third Wave

More years went by. Eventually, the market recovered. There was a period of calm. Inevitably, more bad news arrived on the television and in the newspapers (remember that this was pre Internet). Again, it was the kind of bad news that during the good times would simply create a hiccup on the stock market charts, but now it morphed into the third major market slide. After all this time, though, only the most patient and stalwart investors were still in the market. They generally represented a class of "market savvy" investors with the deepest pockets. They now had finally become impatient with the lack of anticipated gains or the experience of continued losses. They started to capitulate and sell into the third drop. Unfortunately, because there was more money selling into this drop than ever before, a third drop, even larger than the second, became the reality.

Two Important Questions

1.) Did everyone who lived through this third wave panic?

The answer: No. Some people actually stayed fully invested in the market from 1966 to 1982. Their reward: zero, zilch, nada!

2.) Who do you think these stalwarts were: the pessimists or the optimists who always thought the recovery was right around the corner?

The answer: The optimists, of course.

If you know any of these people, you might want to ask them, "In retrospect, was it worth it?"

Where Are We Now?

As I'm writing this book in the Spring of 2011, we've been in the secular bear market for 11 years and have already experienced two major dips. We are currently in one of those periods of calm: a moment of wistful optimism. The press and its "investigative" reporters are starting to suggest that the worst is over. Stock market smitten advisors, as well as most of Wall Street, are smiling, beginning to enjoy a surge in fees and commissions.

Look where we would be if we were to examine the 1966-82 secular bear market, and compare it to the last 11 years:

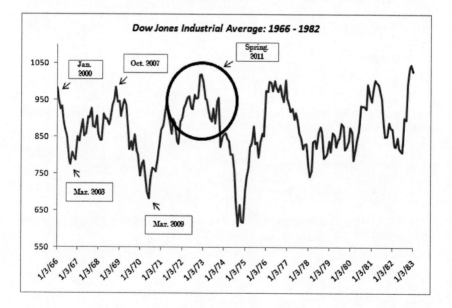

The question you need to ask is can history repeat itself again?

If you tell me that this time will be different, that technology and the ready availability of information make us smarter, savvier investors than any time in history, I would suggest you read Chapter 13. Think about Mr. Einstein's seminal observation, "Insanity is doing the same thing, over and over again, but expecting different results."

If and when bad news starts to surface, it could very well signal the start of a third drop. It actually doesn't matter which piece of bad news starts the market landslide. You can choose any one of the many skeletons that are currently in our country's financial closet. Think about another round of domestic real estate foreclosures, possible municipal debt defaults, foreign sovereign debt defaults, or the specter of the Chinese refusing to buy any more of our government bonds.

As of this writing, there's also a whole batch of potential political landmines just around the corner: the political transitions in Egypt, Yemen, Tunisia, and Jordan; the nuclear weapons stand-off with North

Korea and Iran, and the ever-explosive Palestinian struggle for statehood.

Virtually, any one of these tipping points could start a third major market slide. Again, it really doesn't matter which one. The bottom line is that the last time the market started to slide, we were only seven years into the current secular bear market cycle. Let's say this next slide starts a year from now at the 12-year point. There are going to be investors who have had patience to hold and "hang in there" at the seven-year point, who have now lost their patience and are ready to throw in towel. As we said earlier, those people are often the wealthiest with the larger accounts. When they start to sell into that third drop, it could again very well be the largest.

The Causes of Impatience

There is no specific answer to what causes individual investor impatience to often come in a set of three waves or more. We're all wired differently in that regard. We all become impatient with losses and/or lack of gains at different times. I believe that most of it is due to purely emotional factors. But two tangible factors do come into play: "Your Life Stage" and "Your Risk Tolerance."

Life Stage

Generally speaking, the older you are and the closer to retirement you are, the less likely you are to want to absorb a big loss. Let's create an example in real terms. Bob and Mary had $1 million in assets that they had saved to create a comfortable retirement income nest egg. That plus social security was going to allow them to live a comfortable life style.

Now, imagine that the stock market shrinks their nest egg to $600,000. It's still a lot of money, but that loss might cause a drop in income of 25 to 40 percent. What do you think that would do to their quality of life?

Even if you assume that they can create gains of 67 percent or more to offset those losses by "hanging in there," it will take considerable time to recover. If they are drawing on those assets during that time, they'll need yet a greater return and more time to recover.

Unlikely scenario? Too pessimistic? Never happen? Witness March of 2009, when the S&P 500 bottomed out below 700 points and the DOW bottomed out below 7000 points. Even if there is a third drop in the stock market that merely matches that second drop (let alone exceeds it), that will still destroy a significant amount of wealth for American investors who are retired or approaching retirement.

While panic is never pleasant, it usually has an underlying rationality. Suppose you happened to be seriously planning retirement during this drop. You would have looked at the negative market trends and asked yourself, "Do I want to take a chance losing more of my lifetime assets, or should I fish and cut bait before it's too late?"

Tolerance for Risk vs. Common Sense

Now let's talk about younger investors on the other end of the spectrum. They have the time to recover, so logically they would have a higher tolerance for risk. Even then, there are certain realities. If you've experienced a 50 percent decline in the value of your assets, it will require a gain of 100 percent just to break even. Do you keep swilling the Kool-Aid and let the money ride? Few do.

Let me ask you a question: Do logical people enjoy taking risks just for the sake of taking risks if there is no potential reward? I could box Mike Tyson for one round, and I probably wouldn't die; the wounds would most likely heal, eventually. But, why would I do that to myself if there were no potential reward? On the other hand, if someone were to pay me a purse of $10 million to withstand the beating, I'd at least have to think about it! Do you get my point?

I believe that the financial world has done you as an investor and me as an advisor a disservice. Why? Because they taught us that the major determinant of how much risk an investor should take depends primarily upon his/her "Risk Tolerance Level." They have completely ignored what I believe should be a second major factor: whether or not that investor is likely to get rewarded for that risk. Right now, if you believe that history repeats itself, the answer is: You probably won't.

So, an investor can continue to cross his/her fingers and toes and hope for growth in spite of nearly 200 years of market history. My concern is that instead of an orderly build of assets, he/she might experience shrinkage instead, with its accompanying heart pounding ups and downs.

So what other options does that young investor have? Seek income, not growth. Even if that individual will not need to receive income from the portfolio for years to come, that income can be reinvested to create growth organically and with much more predictability. I call it "Growth, the Old-Fashioned Way"

As I write this, I'm 45 years of age. I'm at a life stage that allows me the time to recover from major stock losses. However, I have elected not to participate in the stock market roller coaster ride because I believe that history repeats itself for a reason, and I am only willing to take risks when I think there is a reasonable chance of reward. My assets are growing nicely; I will be in good shape if I ever decide to retire, and I'm enjoying life now because I have peace of mind. Is that so bad?

Chapter 9

The Facts, a Summary

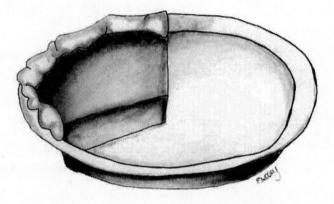

1. Never forget that a 50 percent market drop requires a 100 percent gain to merely break even. In addition, while you're waiting for that recovery, you are earning nothing, like in zilch! When you factor in inflation, it's much worse.

2. Generally speaking, it takes about 35 years for the market to go full cycle. Now you know the actual definition of "long run" when an investment

broker suggests the market outperforms other investments in the long run.

3. Over the last two centuries, virtually every secular bull and bear market has lasted 15-20 years. Occasionally, the bulls have been a little shorter and the bears a little longer. I believe that it's unlikely this pattern will change anytime soon.

4. Beware! Wall Street and most of the financial world prefer to talk in terms of shorter-term cyclical cycles as opposed to longer term secular cycles because it can talk about "recoveries" and speak optimistically more often.

5. When it comes to *your* hard-earned dollars, if the cyclical bulls and bears negate each other, resulting in zero growth, then you've indeed experienced a secular bear market cycle.

6. At the end of most secular bull market cycles, price to earnings ratios have been at or above 30. Conversely, we typically don't recover from a secular bear market cycle until P/E ratios are in the single digits.

7. Corporate earnings would typically have to quadruple for P/E ratios to drop from over 30 to under 10. How long does that take? History suggests typically about 15-20 years.

8. The average investor is only active in the financial markets about 35 years before he/she reaches life expectancy. That's why I believe each generation repeats the same mistakes, rather than learns from the lessons of history. Specifically, the mistake to which I'm referring is to permit "personal greed" to create speculative bubbles and, therefore, self-fulfilling 35-year cycles.

9. "Buy and hold" works better in a secular bull market cycle while in a secular bear market it insures zero growth accompanied by volatility for long periods. If this philosophy is good enough for Warren Buffet, it's good enough for me!

10. Beware again! Wall Street likes to talk in terms of business cycles rather than secular market cycles. Why? It can talk about "recoveries" and speak optimistically, more often.

11. It's very common for secular bear markets to have three or more major down waves, each larger than the previous. At this writing, in the Spring of 2011, we've only had two down waves within the current secular bear market. Hmmmmmm....

Part Two

The Bull

Why you don't know all the facts.

Financial Insanity

Chapter 10

Wall Street Bull

*"Full of Bull. Do what Wall Street does, not what it says,
to make money in the market."*

~Stephen McClellan
Author of the book
"Full of Bull"

Ever wonder why the Wall Street Bull is a world-wide icon. Think about it. What does it imply? Strength? Power? Growth? If you owned the New York Stock Exchange, wouldn't that be the image you wanted to project? If you were the CEO of a publicly-traded company, wouldn't you want to list your company's stock on that exchange? Isn't that an organization with which you'd want to do business?

Shareholder Value Bull

And, so it is that every Wall Street CEO has a little bull in him. Most Wall Street firms will say that their number one priority is to help you grow your money. But do you know where the defined fiduciary responsibility of a Wall Street CEO lies? It lies with the firm's shareholders, NOT you, the investor or account holder! In fact, his/her directive, handed down from the board of directors, is to "maximize shareholder value." So, ironically, your priorities are better aligned with the firm's as a stockholder of that company than as a customer!

But think about that statement for a minute. How can the aforementioned CEO increase share-holder value? He must increase profits to his firm.

How? The first step would be to gain and retain customers. The second would be to keep them fully invested in the markets as much as possible. Otherwise, revenues from stock trades and/or fees go down, and shareholder value decreases.

In general, do you think that people are more apt to stay fully invested in the markets when they are optimistic or pessimistic about the future of the markets? A rhetorical question, of course. So, out of necessity, the primary goal of Wall Street leadership is to speak optimistically as often as possible. That's one of the reasons it's easier for them to hang their hat on shorter-term, cyclical cycles than longer-term, secular cycles. I believe it is also why they focus on business cycles rather than stock market cycles.

Suppose the CEO of one of the major investment houses, back in the year 2000, announced to all of his/her brokers, the entire sales force, that we were entering a 15-20 year secular bear market; this would result in zero growth over that period accompanied by a ton of volatility. Suppose he then stated that they shouldn't put their customers in any more stocks or mutual funds during that period.

Do you realize the impact on corporate profitability? Do you think that the board of directors might fire him and replace him with a more optimistic CEO who is willing to sell optimism to its sales force?

Executive Bull

There is also a far more personal reason to keep you believing. Broad scale investor reluctance would cause enormous pain in the personal pocket book of the CEO and his other top executives. It's been well documented that Wall Street executives are awarded enormous end-of-year bonuses, regardless of market conditions. That doesn't mean they make the same amount when the market dips, but they still make a heck of a lot! How is that possible? Yup. They keep the commissions and fees flowing by selling optimism to their sales force. In return, these brokers can cheerfully advise you, the customer, to stay in the market.

Investment Advisor Bull

Now let's talk about your advisor. Let's assume he also is well-intentioned. He wants to use the latest research to make intelligent investment decisions on your behalf. But he's also in business to make a profit. He examines his operating costs. He realizes that doing his own proprietary research is too time-consuming and that adding staff to perform such research is too expensive. Instead, he relies on his brokerage firm or goes to syndicated third parties...parties usually owned in part or whole by the Wall Street brokerage firms discussed earlier. He convinces himself that the research is totally independent and unbiased. A buy recommendation comes out. What do you think he is going to do?

So, how do you think it's possible that we seldom, if ever, hear anyone from Wall Street talk about how consistently repeatable these secular market cycles have been throughout history? How can it be that most people reading this book have never heard about this?

I'm sure that probably every large Wall Street firm has several people in its research departments who have higher IQs than I. I believe that most of them are at least aware of these long term secular cycles and their historical consistency. So, again, you have to ask yourself, "Why don't I hear my advisor talking about this?"

Well, as scary as this may sound to some, I believe that many of them are not aware of the existence of these cycles. How could this be?

Analyst Bull

In the second chapter I mentioned that historical stock market information is readily available only from 1926 to the present. When I looked for information before 1926, I had to perform "raw data" research. It was a bit challenging but certainly wasn't rocket science.

As I said before, I'm sure that Wall Street employs many analysts that are much smarter than I. It seems obvious that they could have done the same "raw data" research that I did; in fact, I believe that many have. Here is my theory:

Many investment brokers rely on their firms for research. During the late 1990s and even later, when handed this information from 1926 to the present, they were easily able to observe two secular bear market cycles. One was 1929-1954 and the other 1966-1982.

Firms knew that their brokers would likely discount the first, the Great Depression, a one-time fluke. They assumed this period could never reoccur because of safeguards which our country now has in place.

What's left? Only one secular bear market cycle, 1966-1982. Can you extrapolate any predictable, repeatable trend from only one event? Of course not. So, the investment brokers threw up their hands and declared that it must have been random! Wall Street smiled and breathed a collective sigh of relief.

Again, selling optimism to the public is paramount to the success of these firms, and most advisors rely on research generated from these firms. As a result, it's no wonder many advisors aren't aware!

Communications Bull

The selling of optimism is part of the Wall Street corporate culture from the top down. Even though some in these research departments may know the truth, that information doesn't necessarily trickle down to the retail investment broker. Ignorance can be bliss for the advisor.......but certainly not for the client. In a secular bear market, everybody tells himself nobody could have done more for you, the valued customer or client. The advisor tells you to "hang in there because the market always comes back." After all, that is what his research department tells him. Without realizing why, he becomes a stock market cheerleader.

Now, I want to be clear that in no way do I consider myself to be a conspiracy theorist. I'm not saying that Wall Street and its advisors are purposely out to harm you. They are trying to do the right thing. But, in the end, it is *just the way it is*. They are not about to change, government prodding or no government prodding.

So are you starting to see why I say that Wall Street is in the business of selling optimism?

The Advisor's "Business Model" Bull

Most people are not do-it-yourselfers. They hire advisors. Theoretically, the advantage is that they are not emotionally tied to your money, so there is a measure of objectivity to their recommendations.

Unfortunately, investors need to apply caution to their selection of an advisor. Many advisors are not as objective as one might hope. Often they are "tied" to a specific Wall Street model. For example, many investment brokers choose to specialize in the more aggressive portion of the investment risk spectrum, e.g., common stock or stock mutual funds.

If you tell them that you want to be conservative, they will oblige by investing in "conservative stocks." This term, of course, is a complete oxymoron because, in essence, you are invested in the "conservative end of the aggressive end" of the risk spectrum. After all, the word "conservative" is just a word with different meanings to different people.

Consider the following: You probably know some *extremely* conservative people who by definition would probably never even consider getting a private pilot's license. However, I would bet that if you asked any commercial airline pilot whether he/she is conservative or aggressive, the response would be "conservative." Why? Compared to his/her friend who is a military fighter pilot or acrobatic stunt pilot, he/she is. Again, the word "conservative" is just a relative word.

The bottom line is that many advisors are "tied" to a specific Wall Street model. In certain market environments, the model might perform well, and in others it might not. During the unfavorable times, these advisors have the ability to change their business model, but most do not. Instead, they stick to that with which they're comfortable even though it may be to the detriment of their clients.

Think about Warren Buffet, the world's most successful investor you met earlier in the book. After making billions and billions with a "buy and hold" strategy, he came to the realization that his model was wrong for the times we live in now.

I find that people have an easier time understanding the business models of various medical professionals than financial professionals. Imagine if I told you that I was experiencing some back pain and sought the opinions of four different medical professionals. All four professionals recommended four radically different types of treatment. At first, you might find that alarming. But, what if I then told you that one was an orthopedic surgeon, another was a chiropractor, yet another was a physical therapist, and the final was an acupuncturist? All of a sudden, it would make sense. They each have different philosophies and rarely, if ever, recommend treatment outside of their realms of respective expertise, much like most financial professionals. For most investors, however, the lines of distinction are not as clear in the financial world.

So, what is the moral of the story? Make sure you pick the right advisor. Don't be shy. Ask about his/her business model and areas of specialty. Worry less about liking them, more about respecting them. Make sure they are what I call an "elite" advisor.

That's one of the reasons I developed a company called the Advisors Academy, where I teach intelligent advisors who are genuinely willing to change their business model how they can really help others and fall asleep at night knowing they've done the very best things they could with their clients' money.

Investment Banking Bull

Here is another great source of income for Wall Street: investment bankers who raise billions and billions of dollars in capital for public companies to grow domestically, expand internationally, diversify their product mix, etc. In fact, many of the most in-fluential Wall Street firms earn more on the investment banking side than on the retail brokerage side. Naturally, their job is also to be optimistic; they are in the business of creating investor demand for the capital instruments being offered.

As I mentioned before, the basis for optimism on the retail/brokerage side usually begins in a firm's research department. They analyze companies, stock trends, etc. and come up with a given firm's buy-sell-hold list for the publicly-traded companies that they follow.

Let's say that you were the CEO of XYZ Corporation, a publicly traded company that was looking to raise more capital. Would you rather choose an investment banking firm that has your company's stock on the "buy" list or the "sell" list? Again, a rhetorical question, of course.

Now, let's shift gears. Imagine you are the CEO of that investment banking firm that's about to close the deal that will help the XYZ Corporation raise the capital. Suppose one of your analysts on the retail side wants to put XYZ on his "sell" list because he is concerned about some changes at XYZ. As CEO of the firm, you know that move would kill your deal on the investment banking side because you would never be able to unload all the newly-issued stock. What would you do? What do you think most Wall Street

CEOs do when they know that their fiduciary responsibility is to the shareholders?

Now I know that investment banks "claim" they have created a "Chinese firewall" to prevent flow of research information between the research department and the brokerage department that sells and trades stocks and other investments to generate revenues. But, the fact still remains that with most brokerage firms, 90 percent or so of the stocks followed are either ranked as "buy" or "hold"; only 10 percent or so are labeled "sell". When there is an active investment banking relationship, the number of "sells"----zilch, nada.

Again, I'm not a conspiracy theorist, and I'm not saying that people are purposely trying to dupe the public, but I am saying that the system underlying the stock market is not designed to benefit the average investor.

My Bull

As I mentioned in the preface to this book, I've got all the credentials to do my own research. However, for the first 12 years in the business, I followed conventional wisdom. I had the typical advisor business model: heavy in stocks and stock market based investments, and light everywhere else. After watching the rampant optimism of the 90's, I thought the market might be heading into another long-term bear market. I decided to do my own proprietary research. The findings, much of which I've already discussed, made me change my investment-beliefsystem and my business model. It was difficult, painful, and lonely. Today, I have an investment model that works regardless of market conditions and oodles of happy, satisfied clients.

Chapter 11

Media Hype

*"Hype can be the best thing in the world,
but too much of it can kill you."*

~Eli Roth

Why a chapter entitled media hype in a book about *Financial Insanity*? Actually, if you think about it for a minute, it makes a lot of sense.

Remember in Chapter 5, The Human Factor, we talked about how optimism abounds during a secular bull market; we think it will never end; we invest more than we should and stick around longer than we should. We also discussed the right brain's inexperience, for most investors, concerning the 35 years it takes to experience a full secular market cycle. Speaking of bulls, in Chapter 10 we talked about the "bull" that originates from the mouths of Wall Street.

Besides these factors, what else do you think affects our investment behavior? It's called media hype.

Think about the financial magazines and newspapers you may have read in the late 1990's. Think about some of the titles of the articles. Did optimism not abound? Were you not persuaded that all was well, and the stock market was the best game in town? Were you getting the impression that you would be foolish not to have a majority of your assets in the stock market? And, what about this "new" thing called the Internet? Chat rooms abounded with myths and tips and other silliness.

Now, are you starting to see why your investment decisions back then may not have appeared so crazy at the time? Optimism abounded despite the signals. P/E ratios were skyrocketing, and history was suggesting a more cautious approach. Still, you were being urged, cajoled, and convinced otherwise by the financial media and their spokesmen.

We also need to realize that media optimism about the market exists even in bad times. How many times since the year 2000 did you read that the markets were going to hell in a hand basket, and you should have put your money in the bank and stop investing? If you were reading the same things I was reading, the answer is "none."

These behaviors are related to our previous discussions about secular vs. cyclical market cycles. Again, focusing on shorter-term cyclical cycles gives investment analysts and the media a permission slip to speak optimistically more often because the next bull run is always just around the corner.

The CLUB

Again, when do people want to invest more? When they're optimistic and think the market is going up or pessimistic and think the market is going down? The answer is obvious.

Wall Street and your investment broker know this, and so do the media! This creates an environment whereby not only does Wall Street think they are in the business of selling optimism but also so does the media. Thus, exists the creation of a "CLUB" and potential accompanying "peer pressure." Think about it. Would you rather read publications that have a negative, depressing tone or a positive, hopeful tone?

You also need to realize that the majority of media revenues come from advertising, not the sale of publications. Who are the majority of advertisers? They consist of brokerage firms, mutual funds, and other members of the "CLUB."

As a result, the "CLUB" thrives on insularity. Do you know where the media do the majority of their research? Do they go to the library or independent research firms? Typically not; they interview analysts who are employed by their advertisers, as well as other members of the "CLUB."

Analysts get significant media exposure these days between TV, the Press, and now the Internet. When was the last time you heard one of them discussing a 15-20 year secular bear market? One of their implicit obligations of firm employment is to help that firm sell optimism. In fact, most analysts know that if they contradict the company line, they run the risk of losing their high-paying jobs.

Maybe now you can see why the do-it-yourselfer treads difficult waters. The "CLUB" makes it very difficult for him or her to find truly unbiased research to make his or her investment decisions.

How about the truly independent financial advisor who does not get his research from the Wall Street firms described in the last chapter? Does the media hype affect his recommendations? Sadly, the answer often is YES; after all, he is human also.

Chapter 12

Simple, Not Easy

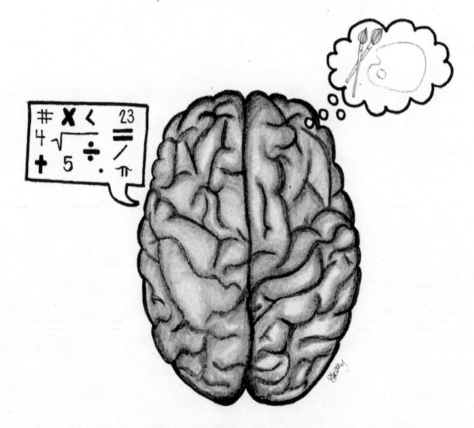

*"People buy on emotion,
then justify their decision with facts."*

~Evan Carmichael
Motivational Speaker

As of late, many books have been written about the science of "behavioral investing." This topic attempts to explain in psychological terms how human emotions affect the financial decisions of investors and oftentimes their advisors.

Several recent studies indicate that, over most periods, the average investor in the stock market earns a lot less return than the market over all. Over the very long term, the stock market averages 9-10 percent return, as we discussed in Chapter 2. Some of these studies say the average investor over this time averages 6-7 percent; others as low as 3 percent. My goal in this chapter is to give you the simplest interpretation I can of why this tends to happen.

The bottom line is that most of us are simply not "wired" to be successful investors. Unfortunately, this statement also applies to most investment brokers.

I like to say that investing is simple but not easy. One has to admit that "buy low and sell high" is a pretty simple concept. However, as human beings, we all have a highly emotional component to our decisions, especially when that decision concerns our life savings.

Most people invest through the "rear-view mirror." Behavioral psychologists call this "hindsight bias," but that's too big a term for me. Only after a big run-up in the stock market do many have the confidence to invest. Unfortunately, they have missed out on most of the gains and have entered the market much closer to the next drop. Often, they invest so late in the game that this drop is right around the corner. Then, the market descent begins. The average investors stay put; after all, they have been trained that the market "always comes back." Only after the drop becomes more significant and the pain is too great to bear do the average investors "capitulate" and sell. Now, this is an exaggerated example, but hopefully you get my point. The end result: "Buy high and sell low," the exact opposite!

In the "old" days, 401k participants were generally allowed to reallocate their funds only on a quarterly basis. As a young advisor then, I had a couple of corporate clients with 401k plans for their employees. Diligently, I would meet with the employees each quarter immediately before the reallocation "window." We would review the various funds and their performance over the last quarter. I would often warn against blindly moving money into the fund that did the best over the previous quarter; I knew from experience that often that fund would become an under-performer in the quarters to come. I'd go back to my office and wait for the reallocation forms to come in. I bet you can guess the outcome. A vast majority of the participants would reallocate in the exact way I warned them against! They would manage their investments through the rear-view mirror: "Buy high and sell low."

Most human beings are more motivated to avoid pain than to seek pleasure. In a word, the stick is more powerful than the carrot. Unfortunately, in life, you tend to get what you focus on.

Success coaches and motivational speakers refer to this as the Law of Attraction. This is the "law" of the subconscious mind which says that we tend to get in life what we focus on. They suggest, for example, that those who want to stop smoking need to focus on how a smoke-free life would look and feel. In other words, they suggest you replace the bad habit with exercise and healthy eating habits. If, however, you were to constantly think about "not smoking," achieving the goal becomes much more difficult.

Why? Because you are focusing on the very thing that you are trying to avoid!

Professional race car drivers know this. They are taught to NEVER look at the outside wall when going into the turn. If they do, their subconscious mind will cause them to drift toward it!

Right now, I want you to pay attention to what I am about to ask you to do. Are you ready? Whatever happens, do not, I mean do not, think of pink elephants. I bet I know what you are picturing.☺

Sir John Templeton, the famous mutual fund manager, has said that a good investor should be a contrarian. That means that one needs to be able to sell after things have gone up significantly and everyone else is still buying. Conversely, one should buy after things have dropped significantly, preferably at a time when most investors are not willing emotionally to pull the trigger and buy. Being a contrarian is simple but not easy.

I hate casinos. I am actually a decent black jack player, but I find gambling to be stressful not enjoyable. My mom, on the other hand, enjoys playing the slot machines occasionally. Several years ago, I took her to a casino for her birthday. After watching her play slots for a while, I became bored, so I took her to the black jack table to teach her how to play. Since it was her birthday, I told her that I would put up my money. If she lost, I would eat the losses, and if she won, she could keep the winnings. So, I asked her to set a goal of how much she would like to win before leaving the table. She looked at me funny. After a few tries though, she finally said that $500 would be enough to entice her to leave the table. So we played. As her winnings accumulated, she didn't know that I was keeping track. Finally, I stood up and told the dealer that we would like to cash out. Mom looked at me like I had two heads; after all, she was winning. I explained that she was up by $515; she could tip the dealer $15 and put $500 cash in her pocket. She exclaimed, "I don't want to quit now; I'm winning!" Luckily, I was able to successfully bribe her with a nice birthday dinner; she walked away with the cash and thanked me later.

Kool-Aid

When it comes to our money, Americans buy gallons of the Kool-Aid called "optimism." As discussed, some comes from the big Wall Street firms, some from advisors who unknowingly are using biased research, and some from the media.

Now, don't get me wrong; optimism is a great quality in the human spirit. Great accomplishments have occurred with the help of optimism. Unfortunately, you cannot will the markets to rise with optimism alone. One irrefutable fact exists: We have been in a secular bear market since 2000. When the tide goes out, all the boats fall.

This is when the inalienable right of all Americans to a "silver lining" rears its head. After all, aren't we the people who built this great democracy from scratch, conquered the West, achieved more than virtually any other nation in modern history? We search for a signal, any signal that the worst is over, and prosperity is right around the corner. We totally buy into the press's cautious optimism (note: Today the press applies to media of all forms, including the Internet). We don't realize that we may be playing a dangerous game of Russian roulette with our hard earned assets. We simply don't understand that we are experiencing a long-term secular bear market. The next "down wave" occurs, and the guillotine again falls on our investments.

Do-It-Yourselfer

Let's spend a minute talking about the do-it-yourselfer. He doesn't believe anybody; he thinks he's too smart for the Kool-Aid. He makes all the final decisions about his money. Ironically, he possesses a blind optimism that he can shelter himself from any financial storm or capitalize on any financial opportunity.

This type of investor typically thinks he is making logical, left-brained decisions and often doesn't realize that because he is emotionally attached to his money, he is dealing with a strong right-brained headwind. When things are going well, greed kicks in. He wants more, faster. When things turn for the worse, fear starts to kick in, and he bails, sometimes irrationally.

No Man is an Island

Don't get me wrong; greed and fear are not bad things when exercised with control. In the caveman days, this "fight or flight" response was very useful in saving lives. Unfortunately, in today's modern world, these emotions can often work against us, especially in the financial world. When you're on an island by yourself, it's hard to know what is the right and wrong decision. The only person you can ask is yourself. As Alexander Pope said in 1492, "A little learning can be a dangerous thing."

Philosophically, that is why many solicit the help of a financial advisor. Theoretically, that advisor should be an impartial third party because he is NOT emotionally attached to your money. The difficulty lies in knowing which ones are truly independent and which ones are drinking the Kool-Aid.

Chapter 13

This Time is Different

"Major economic episodes are typically spaced years or decades apart, creating an illusion that 'this time is different' among policymakers and investors."
~Carmen Reinhart
Senior Fellow
Peterson Institute for
International Economics

Don't get me wrong; optimism is not all bad. It has helped people reach great heights, overcome health obstacles, and invent new things. The concern is that sometimes optimism can go too far and actually cloud decision-making or create the wrong basis on which to make judgments.

Typically, toward the end of a secular bull market, there are a lot of investment analysts who are so smart that they outsmart themselves. They justify their continued optimism by using some rationale to explain that, for the first time, this particular secular bull market will climb indefinitely and go to the moon. Their mantra is, "This time it will be different."

Railroads, Trucks & Planes

During the bull market of the 1890's, the rationalization was *railroads*. The story went like this: Goods could now be transported more easily to points west, so manufacturers could manufacture more, sell more, and make more profits. This is the first time the market was going to the moon in the new Industrial Age.....but it didn't.

In the 1920's, the rationalization was *trucks*. The story went something like this: Now the distribution of goods was not restricted merely to centers near railroad delivery points. Smaller, lighter, more flexible trucks could make smaller deliveries to even the most remote communities, towns, and villages. No American would be left without a broad choice of categories and brands from which to choose. This was the second time the market was going to the moon in the Industrial Age.....but it didn't.

In the 1960's, the rationalization was *airplanes*. The story went something like this: Now the distribution of goods could be provided faster with no territorial barriers. Companies could export their goods and services more efficiently to other countries. This coupled with new manufacturing efficiencies and overhead reductions would explode corporate profits. This was the third time the market was going to the moon in the Industrial Age.....but it didn't.

In the 1990's, the rationalization was *technology*. The story went something like this: Technology has created a new globalization. The world is one. Everybody can sell everything to everybody. New markets will emerge at the speed of light. People, sitting at their computers at home, will be able to purchase goods, and shipping will have a renaissance because virtually everything will be delivered to their doorstep. In fact, some analysts made bold predictions of P/E's of 100 being the new norm. This was the fourth time the market was going to the moon, now in the age of technology.....but it didn't.

As you review the patterns of history, the rationalizations have always been quite similar. "This time it's different" has always meant some form of market expansion or technological improvement. What's going to be the rationalization the next time? Will the analysts be predicting that goods will be shipped in space shuttles to other planets!

Chapter 14

Textbooks Kill

*"Real knowledge is to know
the extent of one's ignorance."*
~Confucius, 512 B.C.

Economics and economic theory have always had a place on the American bookshelf—literally and figuratively.

Client Boxes

As financial advisors, we are taught by our industry (the "CLUB") to put our clients in a box. The financial planning textbooks say that if you are 30 years old, you should have a vast majority of your retirement money in the stock market. If you are 60 years old, the percentage should be somewhere between 30 percent and 60 percent, depending upon when you plan to retire and your personal "risk tolerance." After all, everyone should have some money in the market as a hedge against inflation because people are living longer.

Think for a moment about what that means. If that 30-year old happens to be sitting at the beginning of a 15-20 year secular bear market, he will get zero growth until he is close to age 50. For the 60-year old, he could experience zero growth until age 80! In Chapter 6, we asked a rhetorical question: *"Does getting zero growth on your money for 15 or 20 years in a secular bear market sound like a good hedge against inflation?" You tell me.*

The Rule of 100 and The Rule of 115

These rules are a great example of how we as financial advisors are taught to put people in "a box." If you have talked with "independent" financial advisors recently, you may be familiar with the Rule of 100. It was taught to advisors for decades as a guideline to help them determine the percentage of a person's retirement assets which should be in the stock market based upon his/her age; for example:

% IN THE MARKET = 100 MINUS YOUR AGE

So, the rule indicates that an investor should gradually reduce his/her market exposure with age. Again, a 60-year old would have 40 percent of his/her money in the market, regardless of where we are within the cycle of market biorhythms.

Then, during the late 1980's or so, the "CLUB" started to realize that people were beginning to live longer. As a result, folks should keep more money in the market even at advanced ages as an inflation hedge. The Rule of 115 was born as a replacement for the Rule of 100; for example:

% IN THE MARKET = 115 MINUS YOUR AGE

Now, a 60-year old should have 55 percent of his or her money in the market, regardless of where we are within the cycle of market biorhythms!

As financial doctors, we are killing our patients if we are blindly following the textbooks!

The Stomach Pain

Our historic financial behavior reminds me of what happened to one of my friends. He and his wife were away for a long weekend on their sailboat. They were anchored in a small harbor within an island. He began to have some stomach pain but insisted there was no need to go to the doctor.

The abdominal pains worsened. It was early Friday afternoon, and his wife began to worry. She insisted they return to shore and visit a doctor. They got into the dinghy and motored to the dock. They caught a local cab and went to visit the local doctor. After a long wait, they saw the doctor. The pain had continued to worsen. The doctor said he couldn't find anything wrong.

My friend's wife asked about the possibility of appendicitis. The doctor claimed that my friend was not exhibiting any of the textbook symptoms of appendicitis. He told my friend to take some over the counter pain reliever and see his own doctor on Monday if the pain persisted.

My friend, the ultimate optimist, was all too happy to believe what he heard and was relieved. His wife, on the other hand, was not buying this and insisted they get a second opinion from another doctor. They took a cab to the ferry dock and then a ferry to the mainland. Here they took another cab to the nearest walk-in medical center which was 45 minutes away. They arrived at 5 p.m. just as the primary doctor was about to go home for the weekend. He agreed to see my friend but drew the same conclusion as the first doctor.

Again, my friend was relieved, but his wife was not buying it. The pain was worsening. The night doctor came in, and my friend's wife insisted that he be re-examined. The night shift doctor drew the same conclusion as the other two doctors, but because the pain was worsening, he agreed to admit him overnight for observation. This time, my friend was disappointed and his wife was relieved. By midnight, the pain had gotten so bad that they decided to perform exploratory surgery; after all, he still was not exhibiting the textbook signs of appendicitis. Well, you guessed it: they found a big, red, about-to-burst appendix! When he awoke from surgery, they were both relieved.

The Moral of the Story

1) Blindly following the "textbook" without the use of common sense can kill you.
2) For the men, investing is not a competition sport; stop the machismo. Taking risks when there is minimal chance of reward is ludicrous.
3) Listen to your wife more often.☺

Chapter 15

Monetary Alchemy

*"The difference between genius and
stupidity is; genius has its limits."*

~ Albert Einstein

In the 1950's and 60's, some very smart economists and finance professionals began developing new theories about investing. They were able to "prove" them mathematically and several won the coveted Noble Prize in Economics for their work. This was to bring in a "new age" in investing. One theory was that by mixing together different asset classes (stocks, bonds, tangibles, and cash) in certain proportions, one could reduce risk. This indeed made some sense because one asset class can zig while the other zags, thereby minimizing the overall volatility of the portfolio. It was the magic alchemy to hedge and reduce asset risk.

In the real world, this works MOST of the time, but remember these are mathematically-based, left-brained theories. During the worst of economic times (when investors need this risk reduction the most), these theories often fail. This is what happened from late 2007 to early 2009. During that time, virtually every asset class dropped in value simultaneously.

Very Modern Alchemy

During the 1980's and the 1990's, we experienced the best bull market this country has ever seen. For many college graduates and graduate students, high finance was the growth industry: prestige, glamour, and high income to enhance their lifestyles. *Greed was in!*

Optimism abounded, and as we discussed in the previous chapter, many smart people proclaimed that it would continue, and this time "it will be different." The new, new math of investing was being born.

Some very, very smart economists and finance professionals began developing new, new theories about investing. They theorized that by mixing together different subclasses within the stock market, one could also reduce volatility risk. These subclass pairings included domestic stocks vs. foreign stocks, large company vs. small company stocks, and value vs. growth stocks. Now, investors could remain more heavily invested in stocks (the "CLUB" loves this), but still incur a reduced volatility risk! These very, very smart people then went on to "prove" this mathematically through back testing. The funny thing about back testing is that it can be cloaked in bias. The researcher often tends to find periods which support his/her theories.

Until the year 2000, these theories seemed to hold: One sub-class would zig while the other zagged, thus reducing volatility risk. But, remember that most cyclical bear market cycles inside this great secular bull market cycle were short-lived and weak. Since the year 2000, however, this very modern alchemy failed to hold in most cases.

These "financial physicists," like many scientists, function primarily from their left-brain (see Chapter 12). They make logical, mathematical arguments. Many times, though, they lose sight of the fact that the financial markets are an emotional place. Assets in a free market are priced based upon their balance of supply vs. demand. Demand during "normal" times is logically determined by the left-side of the brains of most investors. During abnormally good or bad times, however, this demand is often emotionally determined by the right-side of the brains of most investors. During good times, the greed kicks in, so the demand increases; this is what happened towards 1999 with technology stocks and again toward 2007 with the stock and real estate markets in general.

During bad times, the fear kicks in and demand decreases; this is what happened during the periods 2000-2003 and 2007-2009. These are times when the mathematical models fail and the "financial physicists" go into hibernation. After all, successful investing is more of an art than a science.

Advisor Gullibility

My trip through market cycles also taught me a lot about other advisors: my competition and my friends. Advisors want to believe the next newest thing will be better than the last. Unknowingly, they turn their clients into guinea pigs by managing their money using these theories. They sell with a false sense of confidence that time will validate that they did the right thing. Another thing I learned is that salesmen are the easiest people in the world to sell. They are constantly being bombarded by wholesalers of Wall Street's newest financial products. An untested theory or a new product with all the bells and whistles packaged properly sounds like a market-proven slam dunk.

Enter Dave

It was during the 1980's when I entered the business. I was going to be the best. I was going to figure out how to get my clients the highest rate of return with minimal risk. My undergraduate degree is in mathematics, so I devoured these modern theories like one drinks cold beer on a hot day. I knew that there were others in the industry who were smarter than I, but I also knew that I could outwork any of them. I studied hard to achieve every voluntary accolade I could. I was seeking the "holy grail" of investing. I eventually became a Certified Financial Planner, a Chartered Financial Analyst, and attained a Master's Degree in the Science of Financial Planning (even the degree contains the word "science") as well as many others. I studied these new, new theories of investing and was confident that risk could be mathematically mitigated.

My Tipping Point

In 1998, I was in the throes of studying for one of the final components in the long list of credentials listed above. I was studying about the theories of several prize winning economists. You guessed it: left-brained, mathematical theories. These economists had become so revered that they were asked to become partners in a hedge fund that utilized their theories to manage the money of affluent investors. Largely behind the reputation of these two economists, this hedge fund had become the largest in our country, long before Bernie Madoff became a household name.

BAM! August 1998 came and this hedge fund hit the newspaper. An abnormally bad thing was occurring: the Russian economic currency was plummeting. Investors were making right-brained, emotional decisions; these highly touted strategies had failed and the fund went under. My world was ruined worse than the day I found out that Santa wasn't real!

In my zeal to excel professionally, I forgot something so basic, so fundamental, I'm almost embarrassed to say it: I forgot about the human factors that influence market dynamics and the herd mentality. I forgot about the irrational behaviors that accompany fear and greed and the inherent sense of optimism that is part of every Americans DNA.

As I watched the market reach dizzying heights in the unforgettable 90's, I started to realize that none of this made sense. A secular bear market had to be on the horizon. The "financial physicists" are wrong; this time it won't be different!

Until now, however, my entire paradigm as a financial advisor, like most others', had revolved around the stock market. I had to research other alternatives that could give my clients a fighting chance of making money in a secular bear market.

Sanity Arrives

And, so it was in 1999 that I began to preach the notion that you don't have to cross your fingers and toes and hope for capital appreciation to increase your net worth. After all, sometimes growth turns into shrinkage. Why not invest in things that generate consistent income, in the form of interest or dividends, and build your assets predictably without participating in the stock market. I refer to it as growing your money "the old-fashioned way."

People laughed...at first. After all, the bull market was still roaring in 1999. I just plodded along, trying to get my message out to those who were open-minded enough to listen. I'm not exactly a flamboyant salesman. In fact, some people find me a little boring.

But, fortunately, boring allowed me to slowly develop a following among sane people who wanted to grow and protect their retirement assets. Since then, I've sheltered hundreds of millions of dollars of clients' hard earned assets, developed a flattering level of peer respect, and made a pretty nice living along the way. That's one of the reasons I decided to write this book. I want investors to get their fair shake. And, I want advisors to realize that there is a better way to build retirement wealth than blindly following the Wall Street Bull.

If you don't mind, I'd like to share a little of my investment philosophy with you. Hopefully, what you've read so far suggests investing in another way may be worth considering. I call the philosophy, "Making Money the Old-Fashioned Way."

I know, it sounds a little boring. But trust me, it works.

Chapter 16

The Bull, a Summary

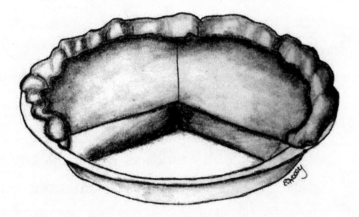

1. The fiduciary responsibility of the Wall Street CEO is to maximize the value of *his* company's stock for *its* shareholders. It is not to maximize the portfolio value of its customers/investors. Often, there is inherent conflict between the two.

2. Wall Street knows that investors are more likely to invest when people are optimistic about the financial markets. So, an important part of its role

is to sell optimism to the public. This "mission of optimism" permeates every level of Wall Street firms from management to the research analysts to the investment broker.

3. The media typically do their "research" by interviewing their advertisers, i.e., Wall Street firms and financial institutions. This unwittingly creates a lethal "CLUB" of optimism. The net result: Everywhere the investor turns, he is being sold optimism.

4. "Buy low/sell high" sounds simple but is not easy to execute. Why? Because human emotions get in the way. Most of us are simply not "wired" to do this effectively and consistently. It's very difficult emotionally to buy "low" when the market has just been through a dramatic down-turn. Conversely, it's difficult to sell when the market appears to be on the rise.

5. Toward the end of every secular bull market optimism causes some "experts" to rationalize that this time will be different, and the market will

continue to rise on its way to the moon…but it never does. Inevitably, the next secular bear market always comes.

6. Most smart investment advisors are taught by our industry, the "CLUB," to identify the amount of stock market exposure a client should have in his portfolio based solely upon his risk tolerance level, i.e., age, without regard to market cycles. The end result? Zero return and lots of volatility for 15 or 20 years at a time. Sound familiar?

7. Over the course of history, some really smart people I call "financial physicists" have attempted to use statistical probability and sophisticated mathematical algorithms to remove the risk from investing in the stock market. Some have even won Nobel prizes for their theories. There is one, little problem …when things go really haywire in the market and investors need them to work the most, they DON'T.

Chapter 17

Tortoise and the Hare, Redux

"There is no such thing as a free ride."

~Shelly Fredman

125

There is a financial rule of investing that is so fundamental, it should be taught the first day of any financial course. Unfortunately, it seldom is.

The Golden Rule: Generally speaking, there are "two ways" to grow your money: *aggressively by taking investment risks or conservatively by committing to a time frame.*

Learn from a Children's Fable?

The hare tries to reach his destination with a confident but reckless abandon. He believes his guile and speed can outrun or outmaneuver any obstacles he may experience along his way. So too it is with the risk-taking investor ("the hare") who follows a course of investing or investment advice that relies heavily or exclusively on direct participation in the stock market. The preceding chapters have explained some of the historical obstacles that one will inevitably experience. Hopefully, if you are using primarily stock market based strategies in your portfolio, you now realize that the odds of achieving your desired financial success are stacked against you.

The tortoise is also equally confident his strategy will allow him to achieve his goal. He believes by plodding along at a consistent speed and staying on a straight course, he will tie or beat the hare because he makes fewer mistakes. Clearly, his strategy is based on an absence of risk.

Risk vs. Time Frame

Again, there are two ways to grow your money: take risk or commit to a time frame.

$$\begin{array}{l} \text{RISK} \xrightarrow{\text{OPPOSITE}} \text{SAFETY} \\ \hspace{4.5em} + \\ \text{TIME} \xrightarrow{\text{OPPOSITE}} \text{LIQUIDITY} \end{array} = \text{MINIMAL\% INTEREST}$$

Why? If you insist on complete safety and liquidity, you have just limited your universe of investment options to banks, money markets, and the mattress. Sadly, as of this writing in 2011, bank deposits are earning less than 1 percent interest.

In other words, the spread between sticking your money in the mattress and putting it in a conventional bank is not that far apart. I know that most people can't possibly reach their financial goals earning one percent.

It Gets Worse

Currently, 30-year mortgage rates are less than 5 percent for someone with good credit. Think about that for a moment.......

Let's say that you have $100,000 in a bank account or a certificate of deposit (CD), earning about 1 percent. You apply for a $100,000 mortgage at a great rate of 5 percent. The bank loves it because it would earn about a 4 percent spread annually on this transaction.

The bank will tell you that the extra 4 percent is to compensate them for the risk of default. Don't believe it! Why? Instead of investing in mortgages, the bank could buy a 30-year U.S. Treasury bond, which theoretically has no default risk and earn more than 4 percent. That makes their real compensation for default risk 1 percent.

So what do banks do with the other 3 percent they have earned on your money? They cover bank overhead and generate profits. It is common knowledge, however, that banks are operationally inefficient.

Banks, particularly the larger ones, promote personal service and convenience as benefits to the customer given today's busy lifestyles.

Isn't it great that in most areas of the country, a bank customer lives within fifteen minutes of a branch office of his bank? Isn't it convenient?

Isn't it also great that each branch is staffed with employees who stand ready to help with your banking needs? Isn't that personal service great?

But, who pays for that service and convenience? You bet: we do. Like most things in life, it comes at a cost. In the case of banks, that cost can be significant as in the example below:

$125/ Month for a Checking Account??

Would you pay that much for a monthly checking account maintenance fee?

Of course not…intentionally.

Let's go back to that example of having $100,000 deposited in the bank. If you are one of the luckier ones, you might be earning $2000 interest this year (I know that no bank is actually paying 2 percent now, but humor me). After you pay taxes on that interest, you might get to keep $1500 or less, depending on your tax bracket. Sound OK to you? Hold on; we are not done yet.

Most estimates of inflation over time are at least 3 percent. Based upon a $100,000 balance, that means that your account is losing $3000 per year of buying power. The net result is an economic annual loss of $1500 ......a monthly loss of $125!

$$\$100,000 \text{ BANK BALANCE} \times 2\% \text{ INTEREST RATE} = \$2,000/\text{YR INTEREST PAID}$$

$$\text{BUT... WHEN ACCOUNTING FOR TAXES } \& \text{ ANNUAL INFLATION.}$$

$$\$2,000 - \$500 (\text{TAXES}) - \$3,000 (3\% \text{ INFLATION LOSS})$$

$$= -\$1,500 \text{ PER YEAR LOSS}$$

$$= -\$125 \text{ PER MONTH LOSS}$$

I don't know about you, but I certainly would be willing to forgo a bit of convenience and personal service to recapture this "bank convenience fee." Remember: *This example assumes an optimistic interest rate and a conservative inflation assumption. In reality, it's worse!*

So what does this mean in the real world? It means that economically you would be better off withdrawing this money and spending it now because it will never be able to buy more goods or services than it can today!

The Good News

Most readers of this book probably don't need as much liquidity as they might think. They have adequate insurance coverage to protect against most financial emergencies. Simply put, they don't need to incur the exorbitant "bank convenience fees" discussed earlier.

Some more good news is that retirement accounts need virtually no liquidity; they just need to generate income. Most retirees wish to live off their interest or dividends and never touch principal. This strategy provides safety, peace of mind, and the ability to ultimately leave some assets to those you love.

In fact, there exists an interesting paradigm when it comes to your retirement dollars. As *a general rule, more liquidity means less income, and a longer time frame commitment means greater income.* Time can be your friend if you're trying to maximize income!

MORE LIQUIDITY = LESS INCOME
LESS LIQUIDITY = MORE INCOME

If you've gotten this far with my book, I know that you are not the complacent type who is satisfied making 1 percent in the bank. Given the first 16 chapters, you are probably also thinking that the stock market might not be the best game in town...certainly not right now.

So, then what is the only other *intelligent* course of action?

That's right: invest your retirement assets using "time-frame committed" strategies. It will allow you to better grow your money without the risks of the stock market.

So, how much of a time frame?

Generally, time frames can range from 5 years to 30 years. Fortunately, most investors don't need to go past 10 or 15 years to get a reasonable return.

For those of you who think that even 10-15 years is long, there is some more good news. First, in most cases, these instruments can begin generating income almost immediately.

Second, most of these instruments can be liquidated before the maturity date if needed; it just means that there might be a penalty or loss if that's the case. A lot of times, though, that is not as onerous as it sounds. Let's say that you invested $100,000 in a conservative, 10-year instrument 5 years ago, but need to liquidate early. Your money has been generating 5 percent interest/dividends, and you've reinvested that income. Your account would be worth $127,628. Assuming you incurred a 5 percent penalty or loss, aren't you still ahead of the game?

Chapter 18

Dull, Boring, and Old-Fashioned?

"Why not deploy traditional solutions to solve modern problems? Interior decorators do it all the time."

~Dave Scranton

We live in exciting times. Technology has allowed us to expand our minds and truly create an interdependent world. Information, shopping, and maintaining social relationships are all available, 24 hours a day, 7 days a week. Sometimes, I almost feel guilty if I'm not texting in the middle of dinner. God forbid if friends think I'm "out of touch."

Why am I bringing this up? Because what I'm about to tell you might be treated with scorn by some of Wall Street's more "modern" analysts and financial advisors. So, you need to be prepared.

More than 30 years ago, conservative financial investment alternatives were extremely popular with retirees and those approaching retirement. Since the last bull market began in the early 1980's, however, they have gotten labeled as dull, boring, or old-fashioned. As a result, most investors today have, at best, a basic understanding of these investment strategies without any real world experience.

My agenda in this chapter is not to teach you everything you need to know to research and choose these financial tools but to give you a general overview of the options. Without any real world experience with these alternatives, I would highly recommend seeking the help of a qualified financial advisor who specializes in them. In other words, *do not try this at home!*

Bird in Hand

With the exception of bank CDs, all of the investment vehicles I'm about to discuss are designed to pay interest or dividends in the range of 3 - 7 percent in today's extremely low interest rate environment (as of this writing in the Spring 2011). Some have no risk of loss if held to maturity, and others have some risk of loss.

Regardless, they are all generally considered to have less risk of loss than common stocks or stock mutual funds. Also, the financial effect of any potential loss in the value of the principal amount is somewhat mitigated by the steady income being received.

Building your wealth by receiving predictable interest and dividends from your investments is what I call the "bird in hand" approach.

Pretty boring, huh!

The Universe of Investment Options

CONSERVATIVE	MODERATE	AGGRESSIVE
CERTIFICATE of DEPOSIT GOVERNMENT BONDS FIXED ANNUITIES INSURED MUNICIPAL BONDS	CORPORATE BONDS INDEXED ANNUITIES PREFERRED STOCK NON-PUBLICLY TRADED R.E.I.T.s	COMMON STOCKS STOCK MUTUAL FUNDS COMMODITIES "SPECULATIVE" REAL ESTATE

On the right are investments that are generally considered to be riskier: common stocks, stock mutual funds, and commodities. People typically buy these for potential capital appreciation, not income. As I mentioned before, though, sometimes you invest for growth and end up with shrinkage.

On the left are safer, insured alternatives such as certificates of deposit (CDs), government and insured municipal bonds, and fixed annuities. Again, they are insured and, therefore, earn a steady interest rate. They are also guaranteed against principal loss if held to maturity. In other words, with most of these, you will know exactly what you will earn over the life of the investment.

In the middle are options such as corporate bonds, preferred stocks, and non-publicly traded

R.E.I.T.s. They have some risk, either because the interest rate can change from year to year or because there exists some default risk of the principal. This group, however, contains investments that are generally considered to be more conservative than the items on the right.

The World of Bonds

A famous poet…, Alexander Pope, once said in shaping political opinions, "A little learning is a dangerous thing." That is also the case with personal financial decision making, which is why I suggested earlier, you may not want to try implementing this strategy "at home alone."

For example, let's discuss the world of bonds. There are many factors to consider when choosing which bonds to buy.

First, one must choose between government, municipal, or corporate bonds.

Second, the financial rating of the issuer must be considered so the investor can determine suitability.

Third, whether the bond in question is callable, convertible, or putable is also relevant.

Fourth, an understanding of certain financial ratios, e.g. coverage ratios, is important; these are often foreign to those who typically analyze stocks.

Last, a final but important consideration in purchasing bonds relates to the direction in which you expect interest rates to change. As a general rule, if you think interest rates will drop, you would favor longer term bonds, and if you think interest rates will increase, then you might favor shorter terms.

How About Interest Rates?

Many people today are assuming that interest rates "have to go up" because they are so low. Certainly, this could be true, but not so fast! In 2007, we had a simultaneous bursting of asset bubbles in stocks and real estate in the U.S. In 1990, this happened in the Japanese economy. At that time, their government lowered interest rates to levels similar to what we are experiencing today. In Japan, rates are still that low today, 21 years later.

Oh, and by the way, their stock market is still at lower levels than 1990!

The Missing Option

You may or may not have noticed that I made no mention of bond mutual funds in the prior discussion. Why? Because in some ways, bond mutual funds have more risk than a diversified portfolio of individual bonds.

Bond issuers make two important guarantees to bond holders. First, they typically guarantee a fixed rate of interest for the life of the bond, and second, they guarantee a repayment of the face amount at maturity (providing there is no default). When you purchase a bond mutual fund, however, you receive neither of those two guarantees. The interest/dividend rate on a bond mutual fund can fluctuate, and there is no fixed maturity date at which you are guaranteed any fixed repayment of principal.

Yes, owning a bond mutual fund may be a simpler way to diversify in the bond market; but, as I've said before, simplicity usually comes at a cost!

The World of Preferreds

"Preferred Stocks" are confusing to some because technically, they represent a different class of stock (compared to "regular" stocks which, as you know, are called common stock). However, they have many bond-like attributes. I personally think of preferred stocks as being more bond-like than stock-like.

Why? For one thing, they pay a stated, consistent dividend rate much like bonds. Secondly, they tend to fluctuate in value more with the corporate bond market than the overall stock market. The dividend is typically higher than the interest rate in a "comparable" corporate bond; this higher rate exists to compensate investors for the added risk. Although the dividend rate is not guaranteed per se, it tends to be very "sticky." Corporations will drop dividend rates on common stock but typically not on preferreds unless as a last resort before defaulting on debt.

They are more stock-like because in the case of a corporate bankruptcy, bond holders have an opportunity for a partial repayment of principal before holders of preferreds. Also, preferreds either don't have a fixed maturity date or that date is so far into the future that the preferred would probably outlive its holder.

Given the above product characteristics, the inclusion of preferreds in a retirement portfolio should be subject to similar analysis to corporate bonds but with a few added elements.

The World of Annuities

There has been a lot of press lately about annuities. Some is favorable, but a lot is unfavorable. I believe strongly that most of the unfavorable press originates with members of the "CLUB." Since annuities are offered by insurance companies, every dollar in an annuity is not in the hands of Wall Street; it is that simple. Besides, I believe that the "CLUB" likes to attach itself to great American pastimes: not baseball or hotdogs or apple pie but hating insurance companies. ☺

To be fair, though, given the various types of annuities being offered today and all the optional bells and whistles, it is only natural there can be both consumer and professional confusion. After all, some annuity contracts can be almost as overwhelming as a mutual fund prospectus!

Some annuities contain the risk of loss of principal even if held to maturity, others do not. Some have fees, others do not. At their core, annuities are designed to generate income to the annuity holder now or in the future. If you plan to cash out your annuity for a lump-sum expense down the road, an annuity is probably not the best tool for you.

In summary, like anything else, annuities consist of the good, the bad, and the ugly.

The World of Real Estate Investment Trusts

One could consider REIT'S to be by far the riskiest of the items in the middle category. In fact, I feel as though I'm taking some literary license by putting them there.

These are non-liquid real estate based investments that come in many different forms. They often pay very respectable dividend yields, which is why I took the literary license to place them in the middle category.

However, it is important to understand that the risk of loss to principal with real estate is every bit as great as in the stock market. If the real estate is purchased by the R.E.I.T. with the help of leverage, then the risk to principal can be even greater.

There are many things to consider when contemplating an investment in a R.E.I.T. The prospectuses can be even more complicated than those of a mutual fund. That being said, R.E.I.T.'s can still be good investments for the right type of person and for a reasonable percentage of an investor's assets.

The Bottom Line

All the options discussed above are designed to generate consistent income with substantially less risk than common stocks or stock mutual funds. This income can provide cash flow for the retiree or be reinvested to obtain growth the "old fashioned way."

However, I can't stress enough that if you don't have real world experience with these options, you should *absolutely, positively not try this at home.*

The Bottom, Bottom Line

Stop the *Financial Insanity!* There is no such thing as the "absolutely perfect financial vehicle." Whenever people tell me that they heard an advisor make that claim, I usually recommend that they take their wallet and run, not walk, run in the opposite direction. Conversely, when someone claims that no one should ever own a particular investment, I would also shy away. Extreme statements one way or another are seldom accurate; in life, the truth usually lies somewhere in the middle. By definition, no financial vehicle is all bad or all good. If it were all bad, it couldn't continue to exist. If it were all good, everyone would own it!

Chapter 19

Apostles of Change

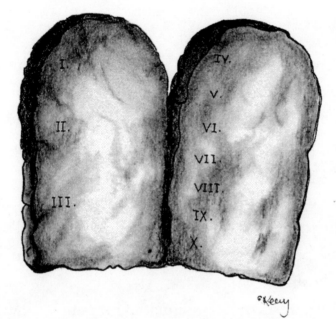

"Insanity is doing the same thing, over and over again, but expecting different results."
~Albert Einstein

I believe every investor should take the business of investing his/her money seriously. After all, most of us spend the better part of our lifetime working to insure that we have the means to enjoy the *second phase* of our life. I call it the second phase because most people, as they get older, are doing something beyond just retiring in the traditional sense. Just sitting around telling stories of our youth, as we calcify from inactivity, is inconceivable to most of us. Getting older can be extremely rewarding; sometimes we decide to give back to society and our community, sometimes we decide to travel the world, and sometimes we decide to start a new business or even a new career.

Spiritualists believe that personal well-being and independence of choice lead to a happy, full life. I believe people also require a strong measure of fiscal good health.

With respect to maintaining optimum health, I believe the world famous integrative medicine practioner, Doctor Andrew Weil, said it best, "Western Society has undergone a philosophical metamorphosis. Today people expect to enjoy a high quality of life as long as they can and then want the end to come as quickly and as painlessly as possible." If you haven't read it, I heartily recommend Dr. Weil's book *Eating Well for Optimum Health*.

With respect to the accumulation and use of wealth, 24 years as a financial advisor has taught me a lot; although money isn't everything, it sure makes life a lot more enjoyable! In my experience, achieving and maintaining optimum fiscal health revolves around my *10 Commandments:*

1. Understand how portfolio loss really works. A 50 percent loss in a particular period will eventually require a gain of 100 percent just to break even!

2. Understanding historical stock market cycles provides valuable lessons learned about their predictability.

3. There is no law which says you have to have any money in the stock market during a secular bear market cycle.

4. Question everything you hear from the financial community and/or read in the financial press. Don't automatically assume it's correct merely because it's in print.

5. Blindly following the financial planning text-books without a strong dose of common sense can kill.

6. Know how much of a risk-taker YOU ARE NOT...before you learn the hard way.

7. Understand as an investor that your emotions may work against you. Remain emotionally detached, or have a third party that you can rely upon for an objective second opinion.

8. Fiscal independence is about making money the old fashioned way...through interest and dividends rather than crossing your fingers and hoping for capital appreciation.

9. Make sure your advisor and his/her team have the experience to do independent, unbiased research or at least the sense to recognize when the research of others is not.

10. Avoid the inflexible advisor who is married to a particular business model, regardless of market conditions.

The Power of Leverage

As I've mentioned on a few occasions, I've spoken to well over 10,000 people during my career about the concepts in this book. For that I am grateful. I've also helped lots of people achieve their financial dreams. For that I am also grateful. Fortunately, God has given me the health and desire to want to continue to help others. But there is a problem. It's called *time*.

I have come to realize that no matter how many people I speak in front of, it will always be a drop in the bucket compared to the number of people that I'd like to help.

I did some math a few years back. I realized that if I should work another 20 years at the same intense pace I am currently working, the facts in this book would have been exposed to only 0.01 percent of the American population that could use help with its retirement planning.

So, I decided to tackle the problem head on. I would use the power of leverage. First, I wrote this book. Second, I created an organization called The Advisors Academy for those elite financial advisors all across America who share my beliefs and are willing to make it their mission to help others avoid all the "bull" and stop the *Financial Insanity*.

I also decided I wasn't looking for the advisor who was looking for a quick fix to expand his practice. No glad-handers. I only wanted to offer Academy membership to serious producers who wanted to offer intelligent, common sense solutions.

It took me a long time to get it right. It took years of study, years of questioning, and years of proving my theories. If I were going to invest my time helping financial advisors do the right things, they would have to be the right advisors who are in this business for the right reasons.

Well, it's four years later, and I'm happy to report that there are now over 150 certified Advisors Academy members all across the United States. They are the best of the best. And, each week we talk to another hundred to find that one special professional.

Once we find that proverbial, quality needle in a haystack, our work has just begun. Each advisor goes through a rigorous course of group as well as one-on-one training. Like any other true professional, he or she is also obligated to remain current by attending our various study groups and work sessions.

So, if you decide to seek out an Academy Advisor or are merely looking for a second opinion about your investment plan, you are guaranteed objective, intelligent insights for you and your family's particular situation.

Financial Insanity

Chapter 20

Summing Reality

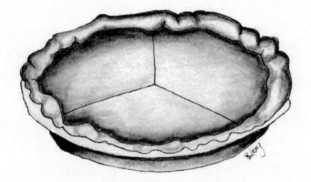

1. Fundamentally, investors have three options:
   a. Invest in financial instruments that deliver safety and liquidity but do not keep pace with inflation.

   b. Invest in risky investments that maintain liquidity but can experience value shrinkage of up to 50 percent or more if the market takes a major drop.

      c. Invest in conservative time-frame committed options, designed to generate interest or dividend income currently in the range of 3 to 7 percent.

2. The third option is the only one where you are not crossing your fingers and hoping for growth or capital appreciation. Instead, you are investing to earn consistent income or dividends in what I call the "bird in hand" approach.

3. There are two possible categories within my "old fashioned" income generating investment strategy:

      a. Invest in fully insured vehicles and receive 3 to 4 percent range of returns (as of this writing, Spring 2011).

      b. Take a little bit of risk, and have the option to obtain a 4 to 7 percent rate of return. (as of this writing, Spring 2011).

4. For most people, a combined approach is probably the most appropriate because no one solution is the right answer for all of someone's money.

5. When selecting an advisor, make sure that he or she has market-proven experience with income-generating, non-stock market alternatives. In other words, fully investigate his/her business model to insure it works in *your* best interest.

Thank You

- I'd like to thank you, the reader, for your time.
- I'd like to thank all the people who helped make this book a reality.
- I'd like to thank all the clients who have put their faith in me.
- I'd like to thank all our certified advisors for speaking the gospel.
- I'd like to thank my friends on Wall Street. Without their gift of greed, there would be no reason to stop the *Financial Insanity*.